Book Design by:
Big Idea Publications © 2014

ISBN: 978-0692314180

IMPORTANT EMAIL ADDRESSES

	Password (if applicable)
EMAIL ______	______
EMAIL ______	______
EMAIL ______	______
EMAIL ______	______
EMAIL ______	______
EMAIL ______	______
EMAIL ______	______
EMAIL ______	______
EMAIL ______	______
EMAIL ______	______
EMAIL ______	______
EMAIL ______	______
EMAIL ______	______
EMAIL ______	______
EMAIL ______	______

IMPORTANT EMAIL ADDRESSES

		Password (if applicable)
EMAIL	______________________________	____________________
EMAIL	______________________________	____________________
EMAIL	______________________________	____________________
EMAIL	______________________________	____________________
EMAIL	______________________________	____________________
EMAIL	______________________________	____________________
EMAIL	______________________________	____________________
EMAIL	______________________________	____________________
EMAIL	______________________________	____________________
EMAIL	______________________________	____________________
EMAIL	______________________________	____________________
EMAIL	______________________________	____________________
EMAIL	______________________________	____________________
EMAIL	______________________________	____________________
EMAIL	______________________________	____________________

WEBSITES

Social Media, Shopping, Personal Interest, Informational, Etc.

Web Address

User Name

Password(s)

NOTES

Web Address

User Name

Password(s)

NOTES

Web Address

User Name

Password(s)

NOTES

A

A

Web Address

User Name

Password(s)

NOTES

Web Address

User Name

Password(s)

NOTES

Web Address

User Name

Password(s)

NOTES

Web Address

User Name

Password(s)

NOTES

Web Address

User Name

Password(s)

NOTES

Web Address

User Name

Password(s)

NOTES

A

A

Web Address

User Name

Password(s)

NOTES

Web Address

User Name

Password(s)

NOTES

Web Address

User Name

Password(s)

NOTES

Web Address

User Name

Password(s)

NOTES

Web Address

User Name

Password(s)

NOTES

Web Address

User Name

Password(s)

NOTES

A

A

Web Address

User Name

Password(s)

NOTES

Web Address

User Name

Password(s)

NOTES

Web Address

User Name

Password(s)

NOTES

Web Address

User Name

Password(s)

NOTES

Web Address

User Name

Password(s)

NOTES

Web Address

User Name

Password(s)

NOTES

B

B

Web Address

User Name

Password(s)

NOTES

Web Address

User Name

Password(s)

NOTES

Web Address

User Name

Password(s)

NOTES

Web Address

User Name

Password(s)

NOTES

Web Address

User Name

Password(s)

NOTES

B

Web Address

User Name

Password(s)

NOTES

B

Web Address

User Name

Password(s)

NOTES

Web Address

User Name

Password(s)

NOTES

Web Address

User Name

Password(s)

NOTES

Web Address ______________________________

User Name ______________________________

Password(s) ______________________________

____

____

NOTES

Web Address ______________________________

User Name ______________________________

Password(s) ______________________________

____

____

NOTES

Web Address ______________________________

User Name ______________________________

Password(s) ______________________________

____

____

NOTES

B

B

Web Address

User Name

Password(s)

NOTES

Web Address

User Name

Password(s)

NOTES

Web Address

User Name

Password(s)

NOTES

Web Address

User Name

Password(s)

NOTES

Web Address

User Name

Password(s)

NOTES

Web Address

User Name

Password(s)

NOTES

C

C

Web Address

User Name

Password(s)

NOTES

Web Address

User Name

Password(s)

NOTES

Web Address

User Name

Password(s)

NOTES

Web Address

User Name

Password(s)

NOTES

Web Address

User Name

Password(s)

NOTES

C

Web Address

User Name

Password(s)

NOTES

C

Web Address

User Name

Password(s)

NOTES

Web Address

User Name

Password(s)

NOTES

Web Address

User Name

Password(s)

NOTES

Web Address

User Name

Password(s)

NOTES

Web Address

User Name

Password(s)

NOTES

Web Address

User Name

Password(s)

NOTES

C

C

Web Address

User Name

Password(s)

NOTES

Web Address

User Name

Password(s)

NOTES

Web Address

User Name

Password(s)

NOTES

Web Address

User Name

Password(s)

NOTES

Web Address

User Name

Password(s)

NOTES

Web Address

User Name

Password(s)

NOTES

D

D

Web Address

User Name

Password(s)

NOTES

Web Address

User Name

Password(s)

NOTES

Web Address

User Name

Password(s)

NOTES

Web Address

User Name

Password(s)

NOTES

Web Address

User Name

Password(s)

NOTES

D

Web Address

User Name

Password(s)

NOTES

D

Web Address

User Name

Password(s)

NOTES

Web Address

User Name

Password(s)

NOTES

Web Address

User Name

Password(s)

NOTES

Web Address

User Name

Password(s)

NOTES

Web Address

User Name

Password(s)

NOTES

Web Address

User Name

Password(s)

NOTES

D

Web Address

User Name

Password(s)

NOTES

D

Web Address

User Name

Password(s)

NOTES

Web Address

User Name

Password(s)

NOTES

Web Address

User Name

Password(s)

NOTES

Web Address

User Name

Password(s)

NOTES

E

Web Address

User Name

Password(s)

NOTES

E

Web Address

User Name

Password(s)

NOTES

Web Address

User Name

Password(s)

NOTES

Web Address

User Name

Password(s)

NOTES

Web Address

User Name

Password(s)

NOTES

Web Address

User Name

Password(s)

NOTES

E

Web Address

User Name

Password(s)

NOTES

E

Web Address

User Name

Password(s)

NOTES

Web Address

User Name

Password(s)

NOTES

Web Address

User Name

Password(s)

NOTES

Web Address

User Name

Password(s)

NOTES

Web Address

User Name

Password(s)

NOTES

Web Address

User Name

Password(s)

NOTES

E

E

Web Address

User Name

Password(s)

NOTES

Web Address

User Name

Password(s)

NOTES

Web Address

User Name

Password(s)

NOTES

Web Address

User Name

Password(s)

NOTES

Web Address

User Name

Password(s)

NOTES

Web Address

User Name

Password(s)

NOTES

F

F

Web Address

User Name

Password(s)

NOTES

Web Address

User Name

Password(s)

NOTES

Web Address

User Name

Password(s)

NOTES

Web Address

User Name

Password(s)

NOTES

Web Address

User Name

Password(s)

NOTES

F

Web Address

User Name

Password(s)

NOTES

F

Web Address

User Name

Password(s)

NOTES

Web Address

User Name

Password(s)

NOTES

Web Address

User Name

Password(s)

NOTES

Web Address

User Name

Password(s)

NOTES

Web Address

User Name

Password(s)

NOTES

Web Address

User Name

Password(s)

NOTES

F

F

Web Address

User Name

Password(s)

NOTES

Web Address

User Name

Password(s)

NOTES

Web Address

User Name

Password(s)

NOTES

Web Address

User Name

Password(s)

NOTES

Web Address

User Name

Password(s)

NOTES

Web Address

User Name

Password(s)

NOTES

G

Web Address

User Name

Password(s)

NOTES

Web Address

User Name

Password(s)

NOTES

Web Address

User Name

Password(s)

NOTES

Web Address

User Name

Password(s)

NOTES

Web Address

User Name

Password(s)

NOTES

Web Address

User Name

Password(s)

NOTES

G

Web Address

User Name

Password(s)

NOTES

G

Web Address

User Name

Password(s)

NOTES

Web Address

User Name

Password(s)

NOTES

Web Address

User Name

Password(s)

NOTES

Web Address

User Name

Password(s)

NOTES

G

Web Address

User Name

Password(s)

NOTES

G

Web Address

User Name

Password(s)

NOTES

Web Address

User Name

Password(s)

NOTES

Web Address

User Name

Password(s)

NOTES

H

Web Address

User Name

Password(s)

NOTES

Web Address

User Name

Password(s)

NOTES

Web Address

User Name

Password(s)

NOTES

Web Address

User Name

Password(s)

NOTES

H

Web Address

User Name

Password(s)

NOTES

Web Address

User Name

Password(s)

NOTES

Web Address

User Name

Password(s)

NOTES

Web Address

User Name

Password(s)

NOTES

Web Address

User Name

Password(s)

NOTES

H

Web Address

User Name

Password(s)

NOTES

H

Web Address

User Name

Password(s)

NOTES

Web Address

User Name

Password(s)

NOTES

Web Address

User Name

Password(s)

NOTES

Web Address

User Name

Password(s)

NOTES

Web Address

User Name

Password(s)

NOTES

H

Web Address

User Name

Password(s)

NOTES

H

Web Address

User Name

Password(s)

NOTES

Web Address

User Name

Password(s)

NOTES

Web Address

User Name

Password(s)

NOTES

Web Address

User Name

Password(s)

NOTES

Web Address

User Name

Password(s)

NOTES

Web Address

User Name

Password(s)

NOTES

H

Web Address

User Name

Password(s)

NOTES

Web Address

User Name

Password(s)

NOTES

Web Address

User Name

Password(s)

NOTES

Web Address

User Name

Password(s)

NOTES

Web Address

User Name

Password(s)

NOTES

Web Address

User Name

Password(s)

NOTES

Web Address

User Name

Password(s)

NOTES

Web Address

User Name

Password(s)

NOTES

Web Address ____________________

User Name ____________________

Password(s) ____________________

____

____

NOTES

Web Address ____________________

User Name ____________________

Password(s) ____________________

____

____

NOTES

Web Address ____________________

User Name ____________________

Password(s) ____________________

____

____

NOTES

Web Address

User Name

Password(s)

NOTES

Web Address

User Name

Password(s)

NOTES

Web Address

User Name

Password(s)

NOTES

Web Address

User Name

Password(s)

NOTES

Web Address

User Name

Password(s)

NOTES

Web Address

User Name

Password(s)

NOTES

Web Address ______________________________

User Name ______________________________

Password(s) ______________________________

____

____

NOTES

Web Address ______________________________

User Name ______________________________

Password(s) ______________________________

____

____

NOTES

Web Address ______________________________

User Name ______________________________

Password(s) ______________________________

____

____

NOTES

Web Address

User Name

Password(s)

NOTES

Web Address

User Name

Password(s)

NOTES

Web Address

User Name

Password(s)

NOTES

J

J

Web Address

User Name

Password(s)

NOTES

Web Address

User Name

Password(s)

NOTES

Web Address

User Name

Password(s)

NOTES

Web Address

User Name

Password(s)

NOTES

Web Address

User Name

Password(s)

NOTES

J

Web Address

User Name

Password(s)

NOTES

J

Web Address

User Name

Password(s)

NOTES

Web Address

User Name

Password(s)

NOTES

Web Address

User Name

Password(s)

NOTES

Web Address

User Name

Password(s)

NOTES

Web Address

User Name

Password(s)

NOTES

Web Address

User Name

Password(s)

NOTES

J

J

Web Address

User Name

Password(s)

NOTES

Web Address

User Name

Password(s)

NOTES

Web Address

User Name

Password(s)

NOTES

Web Address

User Name

Password(s)

NOTES

Web Address

User Name

Password(s)

NOTES

K

Web Address

User Name

Password(s)

NOTES

K

Web Address

User Name

Password(s)

NOTES

Web Address

User Name

Password(s)

NOTES

Web Address

User Name

Password(s)

NOTES

Web Address

User Name

Password(s)

NOTES

Web Address

User Name

Password(s)

NOTES

Web Address

User Name

Password(s)

NOTES

K

K

Web Address

User Name

Password(s)

NOTES

Web Address

User Name

Password(s)

NOTES

Web Address

User Name

Password(s)

NOTES

Web Address

User Name

Password(s)

NOTES

Web Address

User Name

Password(s)

NOTES

Web Address

User Name

Password(s)

NOTES

K

K

Web Address

User Name

Password(s)

NOTES

Web Address

User Name

Password(s)

NOTES

Web Address

User Name

Password(s)

NOTES

Web Address

User Name

Password(s)

NOTES

Web Address

User Name

Password(s)

NOTES

Web Address

User Name

Password(s)

NOTES

L

L

Web Address

User Name

Password(s)

NOTES

Web Address

User Name

Password(s)

NOTES

Web Address

User Name

Password(s)

NOTES

Web Address

User Name

Password(s)

NOTES

Web Address

User Name

Password(s)

NOTES

Web Address

User Name

Password(s)

NOTES

L

L

Web Address

User Name

Password(s)

NOTES

Web Address

User Name

Password(s)

NOTES

Web Address

User Name

Password(s)

NOTES

Web Address

User Name

Password(s)

NOTES

Web Address

User Name

Password(s)

NOTES

Web Address

User Name

Password(s)

NOTES

L

L

Web Address

User Name

Password(s)

NOTES

Web Address

User Name

Password(s)

NOTES

Web Address

User Name

Password(s)

NOTES

Web Address

User Name

Password(s)

NOTES

Web Address

User Name

Password(s)

NOTES

M

Web Address

User Name

Password(s)

NOTES

M

Web Address

User Name

Password(s)

NOTES

Web Address

User Name

Password(s)

NOTES

Web Address

User Name

Password(s)

NOTES

Web Address

User Name

Password(s)

NOTES

Web Address

User Name

Password(s)

NOTES

M

Web Address

User Name

Password(s)

NOTES

Web Address

User Name

Password(s)

NOTES

M

Web Address

User Name

Password(s)

NOTES

Web Address

User Name

Password(s)

NOTES

Web Address

User Name

Password(s)

NOTES

Web Address

User Name

Password(s)

NOTES

Web Address

User Name

Password(s)

NOTES

M

M

Web Address

User Name

Password(s)

NOTES

Web Address

User Name

Password(s)

NOTES

Web Address

User Name

Password(s)

NOTES

Web Address

User Name

Password(s)

NOTES

Web Address

User Name

Password(s)

NOTES

N

Web Address

User Name

Password(s)

NOTES

N

Web Address

User Name

Password(s)

NOTES

Web Address

User Name

Password(s)

NOTES

Web Address

User Name

Password(s)

NOTES

Web Address

User Name

Password(s)

NOTES

Web Address

User Name

Password(s)

NOTES

Web Address

User Name

Password(s)

NOTES

N

Web Address

User Name

Password(s)

NOTES

Web Address

User Name

Password(s)

NOTES

Web Address

User Name

Password(s)

NOTES

Web Address

User Name

Password(s)

NOTES

Web Address

User Name

Password(s)

NOTES

Web Address

User Name

Password(s)

NOTES

N

N

Web Address

User Name

Password(s)

NOTES

Web Address

User Name

Password(s)

NOTES

Web Address

User Name

Password(s)

NOTES

Web Address

User Name

Password(s)

NOTES

Web Address

User Name

Password(s)

NOTES

Web Address

User Name

Password(s)

NOTES

Web Address

User Name

Password(s)

NOTES

Web Address

User Name

Password(s)

NOTES

Web Address

User Name

Password(s)

NOTES

Web Address

User Name

Password(s)

NOTES

Web Address

User Name

Password(s)

NOTES

Web Address

User Name

Password(s)

NOTES

Web Address ______________________________

User Name ______________________________

Password(s) ______________________________

____

____

NOTES

Web Address ______________________________

User Name ______________________________

Password(s) ______________________________

____

____

NOTES

Web Address ______________________________

User Name ______________________________

Password(s) ______________________________

____

____

NOTES

O

Web Address

User Name

Password(s)

NOTES

Web Address

User Name

Password(s)

NOTES

Web Address

User Name

Password(s)

NOTES

Web Address

User Name

Password(s)

NOTES

Web Address

User Name

Password(s)

NOTES

Web Address

User Name

Password(s)

NOTES

Web Address ______________________________

User Name ______________________________

Password(s) ______________________________

____

____

NOTES

Web Address ______________________________

User Name ______________________________

Password(s) ______________________________

____

____

NOTES

Web Address ______________________________

User Name ______________________________

Password(s) ______________________________

____

____

NOTES

P

P

Web Address

User Name

Password(s)

NOTES

Web Address

User Name

Password(s)

NOTES

Web Address

User Name

Password(s)

NOTES

Web Address

User Name

Password(s)

NOTES

Web Address

User Name

Password(s)

NOTES

P

Web Address

User Name

Password(s)

NOTES

P

Web Address

User Name

Password(s)

NOTES

Web Address

User Name

Password(s)

NOTES

Web Address

User Name

Password(s)

NOTES

Q

Web Address ______________________

User Name ______________________

Password(s) ______________________

____

____

NOTES

Web Address ______________________

User Name ______________________

Password(s) ______________________

____

____

NOTES

Web Address ______________________

User Name ______________________

Password(s) ______________________

____

____

NOTES

Q

Web Address

User Name

Password(s)

NOTES

Web Address

User Name

Password(s)

NOTES

Web Address

User Name

Password(s)

NOTES

Web Address

User Name

Password(s)

NOTES

Web Address

User Name

Password(s)

NOTES

Web Address

User Name

Password(s)

NOTES

Q

Web Address

User Name

Password(s)

NOTES

Q

Web Address

User Name

Password(s)

NOTES

Web Address

User Name

Password(s)

NOTES

Web Address

User Name

Password(s)

NOTES

Web Address

User Name

Password(s)

NOTES

Q

Web Address

User Name

Password(s)

NOTES

Q

Web Address ______________________

User Name ______________________

Password(s) ______________________

____

____

NOTES

Web Address ______________________

User Name ______________________

Password(s) ______________________

____

____

NOTES

Web Address ______________________

User Name ______________________

Password(s) ______________________

____

____

NOTES

Web Address

User Name

Password(s)

NOTES

Web Address

User Name

Password(s)

NOTES

R

Web Address

User Name

Password(s)

NOTES

R

Web Address

User Name

Password(s)

NOTES

Web Address

User Name

Password(s)

NOTES

Web Address

User Name

Password(s)

NOTES

Web Address

User Name

Password(s)

NOTES

Web Address

User Name

Password(s)

NOTES

R

Web Address

User Name

Password(s)

NOTES

R

Web Address

User Name

Password(s)

NOTES

Web Address

User Name

Password(s)

NOTES

Web Address

User Name

Password(s)

NOTES

Web Address

User Name

Password(s)

NOTES

Web Address

User Name

Password(s)

NOTES

Web Address

User Name

Password(s)

NOTES

R

R

Web Address

User Name

Password(s)

NOTES

Web Address

User Name

Password(s)

NOTES

Web Address

User Name

Password(s)

NOTES

S

Web Address

User Name

Password(s)

NOTES

Web Address

User Name

Password(s)

NOTES

Web Address

User Name

Password(s)

NOTES

S

Web Address

User Name

Password(s)

NOTES

Web Address

User Name

Password(s)

NOTES

Web Address

User Name

Password(s)

NOTES

Web Address

User Name

Password(s)

NOTES

Web Address

User Name

Password(s)

NOTES

Web Address

User Name

Password(s)

NOTES

S

S

Web Address

User Name

Password(s)

NOTES

Web Address

User Name

Password(s)

NOTES

Web Address

User Name

Password(s)

NOTES

Web Address

User Name

Password(s)

NOTES

Web Address

User Name

Password(s)

NOTES

S

Web Address

User Name

Password(s)

NOTES

S

Web Address

User Name

Password(s)

NOTES

Web Address

User Name

Password(s)

NOTES

Web Address

User Name

Password(s)

NOTES

Web Address

User Name

Password(s)

NOTES

T

Web Address

User Name

Password(s)

NOTES

Web Address

User Name

Password(s)

NOTES

T

Web Address

User Name

Password(s)

NOTES

Web Address

User Name

Password(s)

NOTES

Web Address

User Name

Password(s)

NOTES

Web Address

User Name

Password(s)

NOTES

Web Address

User Name

Password(s)

NOTES

Web Address

User Name

Password(s)

NOTES

T

T

Web Address

User Name

Password(s)

NOTES

Web Address

User Name

Password(s)

NOTES

Web Address

User Name

Password(s)

NOTES

Web Address

User Name

Password(s)

NOTES

Web Address

User Name

Password(s)

NOTES

Web Address

User Name

Password(s)

NOTES

T

T

Web Address

User Name

Password(s)

NOTES

Web Address

User Name

Password(s)

NOTES

Web Address

User Name

Password(s)

NOTES

Web Address

User Name

Password(s)

NOTES

Web Address

User Name

Password(s)

NOTES

U

Web Address

User Name

Password(s)

NOTES

U

Web Address

User Name

Password(s)

NOTES

Web Address

User Name

Password(s)

NOTES

Web Address

User Name

Password(s)

NOTES

Web Address

User Name

Password(s)

NOTES

Web Address

User Name

Password(s)

NOTES

Web Address

User Name

Password(s)

NOTES

U

U

Web Address

User Name

Password(s)

NOTES

Web Address

User Name

Password(s)

NOTES

Web Address

User Name

Password(s)

NOTES

Web Address

User Name

Password(s)

NOTES

Web Address

User Name

Password(s)

NOTES

U

Web Address

User Name

Password(s)

NOTES

U

Web Address

User Name

Password(s)

NOTES

Web Address

User Name

Password(s)

NOTES

Web Address

User Name

Password(s)

NOTES

Web Address

User Name

Password(s)

NOTES

Web Address

User Name

Password(s)

NOTES

Web Address

User Name

Password(s)

NOTES

V

V

Web Address

User Name

Password(s)

NOTES

Web Address

User Name

Password(s)

NOTES

Web Address

User Name

Password(s)

NOTES

Web Address

User Name

Password(s)

NOTES

Web Address

User Name

Password(s)

NOTES

Web Address

User Name

Password(s)

NOTES

V

V

Web Address

User Name

Password(s)

NOTES

Web Address

User Name

Password(s)

NOTES

Web Address

User Name

Password(s)

NOTES

Web Address

User Name

Password(s)

NOTES

Web Address

User Name

Password(s)

NOTES

Web Address

User Name

Password(s)

NOTES

V

V

Web Address

User Name

Password(s)

NOTES

Web Address

User Name

Password(s)

NOTES

Web Address

User Name

Password(s)

NOTES

Web Address

User Name

Password(s)

NOTES

Web Address

User Name

Password(s)

NOTES

Web Address

User Name

Password(s)

NOTES

W

W

Web Address

User Name

Password(s)

NOTES

Web Address

User Name

Password(s)

NOTES

Web Address

User Name

Password(s)

NOTES

Web Address

User Name

Password(s)

NOTES

Web Address

User Name

Password(s)

NOTES

Web Address

User Name

Password(s)

NOTES

W

W

Web Address

User Name

Password(s)

NOTES

Web Address

User Name

Password(s)

NOTES

Web Address

User Name

Password(s)

NOTES

Web Address

User Name

Password(s)

NOTES

Web Address

User Name

Password(s)

NOTES

Web Address

User Name

Password(s)

NOTES

W

W

Web Address

User Name

Password(s)

NOTES

Web Address

User Name

Password(s)

NOTES

Web Address

User Name

Password(s)

NOTES

X

Web Address

User Name

Password(s)

NOTES

Web Address

User Name

Password(s)

NOTES

Web Address

User Name

Password(s)

NOTES

X

Web Address

User Name

Password(s)

NOTES

Web Address

User Name

Password(s)

NOTES

Web Address

User Name

Password(s)

NOTES

Web Address

User Name

Password(s)

NOTES

Web Address

User Name

Password(s)

NOTES

Web Address

User Name

Password(s)

NOTES

X

X

Web Address

User Name

Password(s)

NOTES

Web Address

User Name

Password(s)

NOTES

Web Address

User Name

Password(s)

NOTES

Web Address

User Name

Password(s)

NOTES

Web Address

User Name

Password(s)

NOTES

Web Address

User Name

Password(s)

NOTES

X

X

Web Address

User Name

Password(s)

NOTES

Web Address

User Name

Password(s)

NOTES

Web Address

User Name

Password(s)

NOTES

Web Address

User Name

Password(s)

NOTES

Web Address

User Name

Password(s)

NOTES

Web Address

User Name

Password(s)

NOTES

Y

Y

Web Address

User Name

Password(s)

NOTES

Web Address

User Name

Password(s)

NOTES

Web Address

User Name

Password(s)

NOTES

Web Address

User Name

Password(s)

NOTES

Web Address

User Name

Password(s)

NOTES

Y

Web Address

User Name

Password(s)

NOTES

Y

Web Address

User Name

Password(s)

NOTES

Web Address

User Name

Password(s)

NOTES

Web Address

User Name

Password(s)

NOTES

Web Address

User Name

Password(s)

NOTES

Web Address

User Name

Password(s)

NOTES

Web Address

User Name

Password(s)

NOTES

Y

Web Address

User Name

Password(s)

NOTES

Web Address

User Name

Password(s)

NOTES

Web Address

User Name

Password(s)

NOTES

Web Address

User Name

Password(s)

NOTES

Web Address

User Name

Password(s)

NOTES

Web Address

User Name

Password(s)

NOTES

Z

Z

Web Address

User Name

Password(s)

NOTES

Web Address

User Name

Password(s)

NOTES

Web Address

User Name

Password(s)

NOTES

Web Address

User Name

Password(s)

NOTES

Web Address

User Name

Password(s)

NOTES

Z

Web Address

User Name

Password(s)

NOTES

Z

Web Address

User Name

Password(s)

NOTES

Web Address

User Name

Password(s)

NOTES

Web Address

User Name

Password(s)

NOTES

Web Address

User Name

Password(s)

NOTES

Web Address

User Name

Password(s)

NOTES

Web Address

User Name

Password(s)

NOTES

Z

Z

Web Address

User Name

Password(s)

NOTES

Web Address

User Name

Password(s)

NOTES

Web Address

User Name

Password(s)

NOTES

MISC.

Web Address ______________________________

User Name ______________________________

Password(s) ______________________________

____

____

NOTES

Web Address ______________________________

User Name ______________________________

Password(s) ______________________________

____

____

NOTES

Web Address ______________________________

User Name ______________________________

Password(s) ______________________________

____

____

NOTES

MISC.

Web Address

User Name

Password(s)

NOTES

Web Address

User Name

Password(s)

NOTES

Web Address

User Name

Password(s)

NOTES

Web Address

User Name

Password(s)

NOTES

Web Address

User Name

Password(s)

NOTES

Web Address

User Name

Password(s)

NOTES

MISC.

MISC.

Web Address

User Name

Password(s)

NOTES

Web Address

User Name

Password(s)

NOTES

Web Address

User Name

Password(s)

NOTES

Web Address

User Name

Password(s)

NOTES

Web Address

User Name

Password(s)

NOTES

Web Address

User Name

Password(s)

NOTES

MISC.

Web Address

User Name

Password(s)

NOTES

Web Address

User Name

Password(s)

NOTES

Web Address

User Name

Password(s)

NOTES

Web Address

User Name

Password(s)

NOTES

Web Address

User Name

Password(s)

NOTES

Web Address

User Name

Password(s)

NOTES

MISC.

MISC.

Web Address

User Name

Password(s)

NOTES

Web Address

User Name

Password(s)

NOTES

Web Address

User Name

Password(s)

NOTES

Web Address

User Name

Password(s)

NOTES

Web Address

User Name

Password(s)

NOTES

Web Address

User Name

Password(s)

NOTES

MISC.

Web Address

User Name

Password(s)

NOTES

Web Address

User Name

Password(s)

NOTES

Web Address

User Name

Password(s)

NOTES

Web Address

User Name

Password(s)

NOTES

Web Address

User Name

Password(s)

NOTES

Web Address

User Name

Password(s)

NOTES

MISC.

MISC.

Web Address

User Name

Password(s)

NOTES

Web Address

User Name

Password(s)

NOTES

Web Address

User Name

Password(s)

NOTES

ACCOUNTS

Banking, Credit, Mortgage, Rent, Phone, Cable, Utilities, Medical, Etc.

Web Address

User Name

Password(s)

NOTES

Web Address

User Name

Password(s)

NOTES

Web Address

User Name

Password(s)

NOTES

ACCOUNTS

Web Address

User Name

Password(s)

NOTES

Web Address

User Name

Password(s)

NOTES

Web Address

User Name

Password(s)

NOTES

Web Address

User Name

Password(s)

NOTES

Web Address

User Name

Password(s)

NOTES

Web Address

User Name

Password(s)

NOTES

ACCOUNTS

Web Address

User Name

Password(s)

NOTES

Web Address

User Name

Password(s)

NOTES

Web Address

User Name

Password(s)

NOTES

Web Address

User Name

Password(s)

NOTES

Web Address

User Name

Password(s)

NOTES

Web Address

User Name

Password(s)

NOTES

ACCOUNTS

ACCOUNTS

Web Address

User Name

Password(s)

NOTES

Web Address

User Name

Password(s)

NOTES

Web Address

User Name

Password(s)

NOTES

Web Address

User Name

Password(s)

NOTES

Web Address

User Name

Password(s)

NOTES

Web Address

User Name

Password(s)

NOTES

ACCOUNTS

Web Address

User Name

Password(s)

NOTES

Web Address

User Name

Password(s)

NOTES

Web Address

User Name

Password(s)

NOTES

Web Address

User Name

Password(s)

NOTES

Web Address

User Name

Password(s)

NOTES

Web Address

User Name

Password(s)

NOTES

ACCOUNTS

Web Address

User Name

Password(s)

NOTES

Web Address

User Name

Password(s)

NOTES

Web Address

User Name

Password(s)

NOTES

Web Address

User Name

Password(s)

NOTES

Web Address

User Name

Password(s)

NOTES

Web Address

User Name

Password(s)

NOTES

NOTES

NOTES

Made in United States
North Haven, CT
05 November 2026

21772149R00104